Her Landscape

Poems Based on the Life of
Mileva Marić Einstein

poems by

Catherine Arra

Finishing Line Press
Georgetown, Kentucky

Her Landscape

Poems Based on the Life of
Mileva Marić Einstein

Publisher: Leah Maines

Editor: Christen Kincaid

Cover Art: Tourism photo of the old section of Zurich, Switzerland in winter

Author Photo: Dion Ogust

Cover Design: Elizabeth Maines McCleavy

Order online: www.finishinglinepress.com
also available on amazon.com

Author inquiries and mail orders:
Finishing Line Press
P. O. Box 1626
Georgetown, Kentucky 40324
U. S. A.

Table of Contents

III

My life closed twice before its close—
It yet remains to see
If Immortality unveil
A third event to me

So huge, so hopeless to conceive
As these that twice befell.
Parting is all we know of heaven,
And all we need of hell.

—Emily Dickinson, 1732

Introduction

Mileva Marić Einstein (December 19, 1875–August 4, 1948) was the first wife of the world-renowned physicist Albert Einstein. Until recently, Mileva's life and work have remained shrouded in her husband's rock-star fame. The release of *The Love Letters* and *The Collected Papers of Albert Einstein* within the past thirty years offered new information regarding Mileva's intellectual gifts and her partnership with Albert in both marriage and science. *The Love Letters* in particular precipitated a flurry of new biographies. The 2017 National Geographic TV series *Genius* is based on Walter Isaacson's 2007 biography, *Einstein: His Life and Universe.*

Mileva was a visionary mathematician and scientist in her own right. There is evidence to indicate that she was instrumental, and perhaps a collaborator, in the scientific papers that comprised Einstein's *Annus Mirabilis*, or Miracle Year, of epoch-making theories that redefined the mechanics of the universe and laid the path to his fame. Mileva and Albert married in 1903, after the birth and loss of an illegitimate daughter, Lieserl. They later had two sons, Hans Albert and Eduard. They separated in 1914, and officially divorced in 1919. Despite their sad and tumultuous ending, Mileva and Albert were kindred spirits. Their individual genius and shared defiance of established scientific thought, their unique disregard for convention, their iconoclasm and perseverance, conceived and birthed a bold new universe.

Disorganized and disorderly, Albert needed Mileva to care for him, but more importantly to help him bring his, and their, thought experiments to tangible reality. She needed him to credit her as his scientific partner and to be a faithful husband. Mileva kept her promises, but Albert reneged on his part of the commitment.

This small collection of poems does not attempt to offer biography or argument regarding Mileva's role in Albert's achievements, but does give Mileva a voice in a history that has exalted Albert and left her mute in his shadow. Mileva was a brilliant mathematician and physicist as much as she was an introverted, introspective, keenly intuitive, and above all, kind, woman. She was a devoted mother and wife, who never remarried after Albert abandoned her for his cousin and second wife, Elsa.

Without Albert's willingness to acknowledge Mileva's contributions to their work, her chances for recognition as a scientist amid the institutionalized sexism of the late-19th and early-20th centuries evaporated in the blinding light of her husband's corona.

I

Mileva

His trajectory would span time itself.
His magnetic field, his center of gravity—givens,
a blueprint demanding architects, builders,
fans, financiers, and sacrifice.

He siphoned people into himself, a whirlpool,
or pulled them along in his wake.
Irresistible. His vision unrelenting.
His poetry and light inescapable. All were helpless
against their love, hate, or awe of him.

Each in kind—family,
colleagues, lovers—would become fuel, lift, velocity,
his coterie in collusions, betrayals, all that was necessary
to complete the arc of his life.
It was non-negotiable. No one bargains with God.

I knew his mind, merged and mated with it.
I loved the man too, his boyish frailty,
his appetites and sensuality,
the padding softness of his footfall,
the rhythms of his breathing, his smell.
The way he beckoned me, *come.*

I was his wife. I am Mileva.

Not for Girls

Restrictions are taught,
imposed by family, education, culture. Oneself.

I, a gifted girl born in the Austro-Hungarian Empire
that became Serbia—

a girl with a physical deformity, a prodigious brain for
mathematics and physics.

Papa noticed, nurtured my talents in spite of Mama's insistence
I learn domestic skills. I did both.

Papa pulled powerful strings to give me an
education reserved only for boys.

For Papa I worked hard, for myself too. I loved the malleable magic
of my mind—what it could see and do. I would thank Papa with my success.

Papa loved me with purity that defied boundaries. I too loved this way
and believed Albert when he claimed the same.

Dislocated

I'm not well-liked, so I must be kind, kinder,
and more generous than expected.

I'm the unexpected stranger with suspicious eyes, wary glances,
arms crossed tightly to chest.

A natural posture, you see. I'm warmed this way, protected and secure.
Comforted—the way Papa held me, encouraged me to study, to not be afraid.

A natural pose, not defensive or off-putting as so many surmise.
Albert slouches to his left, right leg crossed to follow; he's at ease this way.

But I'm the dark Serbian, the heavy-footed foreigner who limps and clumps
when she walks, who stares hard into hope with hope.

I'm the witch-woman Frankenstein who dares to be intelligent, a mathematician
who likes to study, who wants what men want, what Albert wants—

to understand the mysteries of the universe,

though the mysteries of human nature prove to be far more crippling than a
bad foot, which, by the way, is a very fine foot at the end of a dislocated hip.

Liebe

What can a woman

with a headful of science, a brain for math,
an intellect of armor,
a steel-edged warrior determination
to study, earn a degree,
rise above commonplace,
to be anything other than common—
the only woman in 1896 to enter
the Swiss Federal Polytechnic,
a candidate for a diploma
and Ph.D. in mathematics and physics, yet
a woman who's never been properly kissed—

do against

the soft-spoken sensual genius,
the barefooted violinist
when he
brown-eyed wooed her, playfully pursued her,
pleaded, placated, smiled, and inched his lips
and breath so close to her cheek, she trembled
and joyfully leapt
into an ocean of flesh.

The Splügen, 1901

—*An alpine mountain pass (6,930' elevation) between Italy and Switzerland, north of Lake Como*

We all look back to a time—
our pinnacle of joy, the peak of health and happiness.

Better this altitude not be too high, for
the depths of sorrow will be proportionate.

After months apart,
our holiday in the blossoming spring
of Lake Como,
up through spiraling tunnels
of Splügen Pass by sled—
my love and I snuggled beneath
shawls and snow—
an exhilarating hike down
to the lovely old city of Chur,
was such a time for me.

In this early May rapture,
my Lieserl* was conceived.

Forces in heaven aligned
to capture Albert and me
in infinite possibilities as well as
a quagmire of trials.

Some call these moments blessings,
while the rest of life becomes
consequence of mundane choices,
stubborn human will.

---

* Mileva and Albert's illegitimate daughter, born in Novi Sad, January 1902. The child died or was adopted in September 1903.

Storms

I'm pulled into a fierce sea,
bullied and bruised by striking waves,
cast down and scraped upon sand and stone.

A shift in humor days before,
a slip in a fault line, a shadow creeping
in with determined stealth, a rising dread.

Other times the torrent arrives unexpectedly,
a fury of frigid wind that augurs winter
on the most delightful autumn afternoon.

Against it, I'm never prepared.
My attempted good cheer helpless,
my chatty letters a ruse.

In stoic defense I study harder,
reach for my *Johnnie*,* aloft on waves above,
navigating sea and stars with ease.

---

* Johnnie and Dollie were the lover nicknames of Albert and Mileva.

The Tug of Gravity

Bern, 1903

I walk the market stalls among fishmongers,
find myself gutted, mouth agape, glassy eye staring.

In my rooms alone, bed pillow pressed to chest, I hold her,
lost daughter, luminous brown eyes searching mine,

infant fingers finding the heart thread that tethers and
weaves a bond, blossoms into labyrinths of bliss and sorrow.

I nursed her, witnessed her sleepy waking to sensation, delighted in her
glee when she recognized my voice, smell, the rise and fall of my breasts.

She is a specter staring back from mirror eyes,
the ghost that follows in long shadows.

The Company of Good Women

I speak aloud
to my dearest friend, Helene,
whisper at night, my truths.
I hear her comforting replies
in sheaths of warmth and memory.

How I long for the company of women,
Helene and Milana, my friends
at the pension in our university days.
How exciting life was then
and how alluring my mischievous young Albert.

My need for women's stillness
is greater now,
when Albert is so occupied with work,
and frequently away from me.
Now, since I've lost Lieserl,
our forbidden angel,
my sweetest self, reaching delicate fingertips
to touch my lips, offering
a smile for her toothless grin in return.

You were taken from me so young, my child—
my delight and demise,
my family's shame, Papa's disappointment, Mama's silence,
the Einstein family's wretched scorn and sabotage,
Albert's dilemma.

II

After Lieserl

I came to think Albert was my destiny.
He, not I, would be the groundbreaker,
the harbinger of new physics.

We married at the Bern courthouse
6 January 1903 and
I devoted all of myself to him.

We were dynamic, moving
as magnetic waves, unraveling mysteries
as if propelled by angels.

Late into nights, after his hours
at the Patent Office, we wrestled out theories,
equations, and the papers of his "miracle year."

Grand men of science who denied me
would know the name *Einstein*,
his vision, the unparalleled reach of his mind.

I willingly worked, melded with him,
and yes, mastered the math. Agility
and discipline manifested things ethereal.

We had another child, Hans Albert.
I never imagined my husband
would leave me.

Pauline

His mother loathes me.
Her vile appraisals began with Lieserl.
Now her poison fills the air we breathe.

She visits to spy, sabotage, bend me
to her ways or prove my incompetence as mother, wife—
certainly not to help with the house and children.

I'm the dark Slav, the non-Jew
with a disfigured hip and ghoulish brow,
far from the pretty blond pixie, Marie,

she would have handpicked for her boy.
How delighted she must have been when
his stay with the Wintelers yielded that romance.

If I were a jealous woman,
I'd envy Albert's beloved science,
not Marie or any commonplace wife. An insult.

Albert will not defend me against
her daily scowls and lectures. He feeds
her disdain, is so much his mother's boy.

She's the thief, the interloping female.
I want his mother gone yet cannot break peace with her.
If she would only embrace, support me …

Doesn't she know
in this world of men
women must help each other?

Stepping Stone

I haven't the gift or propensity
for housekeeping. A frustration.

For as long as Albert needed my calculations,
my research and manuscript proofs,
my honey pot and arms, I was his equal
as much as his stepping stone, though
I did not know it then.

How I imagined we would become
like Marie and Pierre Curie, but my Albert,
he collaborates; he does not share.

1909

His epoch-making *Annus Mirabilis* of 1905 crowned him, made him a worldly man. Mighty scientific minds pursued him (not to mention a few adoring females), begged his company, invited him to lecture.

I was crowned *hausfrau*, swept shadows, waited at windows—his wife nonetheless and pleased for his success, our future, hoping his new fame would not overfeed his self-importance, harm his humanity.

I am again with child.

Don't Misunderstand

I adore my boys,
Hans Albert and little Tete.

It's a wonder
to birth men in a world that works
so masterfully to slight women,
relegate them
to making meals, mending socks, manners.

How I must minimize myself, my merit, and
mathematics to the meticulous mothering of men—
all three.

Thought Experiments / Sex

When a man lives too much in his head,
surveying mindscapes, tunneling imagination,
hallucinating the play of the cosmos,
twisting and bending thought into knots,
only to unravel all and start again,

he can lose footing in the physical world, travel
too far inward, become lost in weightlessness.

He will hike with great vigor the mountains
and hills of Switzerland, exhaust limbs and lungs,
feed his body sausages and sweets,
burrow his sex deep into flesh until balance
between thought and sensation is restored.

Elsa

She pretends friendship, is welcoming, generous.
Sympathizes with my newness to Berlin.
Assists Albert in socializing, forging new alliances.

A darkness is here.
Albert's choice, Berlin. A fine position, advanced prestige.
A husband who has no time for his wife or children.

She pretends scrupulous morality,
sweeping grace, and sleeps with him,
schemes to take him for herself.
Elsa, debutante divorcee with two daughters
and no standing in the world.
Why not steal another woman's husband,
so conveniently her first cousin,
an easy mark, such a prize.

Why does the wishful adulteress
think she knows the man better than the wife?
He will use her too. Another stepping stone.
Another woman who will wait.

Go ahead, pretend.
Convince him he needs you, your connections
and society, your conversation and complement.

But it is he who wants to be seduced and swept away.
It is he.

Gimp

Years of limping, lurching
from one side to the other
have ruined my spine,
twisted it into an arthritic maw.

I welcome bed rest,
possess no will to walk or move forward.
My sons miss my engagement—my sweet boys,
at least I have them.

Gimp, the boys at school
jeered, mimicking when I passed by—
at university in more insidious ways,
though who will ever know if it was my leg or gender
that disconcerted men so. Even mighty professors,
Weber and Lenard, saw it a duty to keep me in my place.

Albert seemed not to notice my impediment,
adored my mind, called me soul mate, his *Dollie*—
my serious countenance reminded him of a porcelain doll.
Such a contrast to his impishness
and outrageous disregard for propriety.

How he pulled me into him,
the glories we imagined we'd create
and the lovemaking.
That slippery oblivion.
Who could resist?

Corseted

I did it for him, for science.
How could I not?
The work was essential
for our future,
the world's.
He insisted sharing his name,
Einstein, *one stone*,
was sharing credit.

And then,
erased in ambiguity,
abandoned for the Elsa-Marie cliché—
women adept at social prancing and prattle,
at using men who use them,
at perpetuating the masculine myth,
oppression, and entitlement
that renders women,
no matter how alluring or clever,
invisible.

How dare he complain of my dark moods,
dismiss my unhappiness.
He used me
not only for the petaled passage between my thighs
but for the infinite possibilities of my mind.
The worst kind of theft.

A volcano pressed between the weight of oceans,
the furnace of Earth's core—I'm wife of the work.

Two of Cups / Two of Swords

Albert to Mileva, August 1 and 20, 1900*

"I long terribly for a letter from my beloved witch. I can hardly grasp that we will be separated for so much longer—only now do I see how frightfully much I love you!"

"Oh my! That Johnnie boy!
So crazy with desire
While thinking of his Dollie
His pillow catches fire."

Albert to Mileva, July 14, 1914**

CONDITIONS

A. You will make sure
>   1. that my clothes and laundry are kept in good order;
>   2. that I will receive my three meals regularly *in my room*;
>   3. that my bedroom and study are kept neat, and especially that my desk is left for *my use only.*

B. You will renounce all personal relations with me insofar as they are not completely necessary for social reasons. Specifically, you will forgo
>   1. my sitting at home with you;
>   2. my going out or traveling with you.

C. You will obey the following points in your relations with me:
>   1. you will not expect any intimacy from me, nor will you reproach me in any way;
>   2. you will stop talking to me if I request it;
>   3. you will leave my bedroom or study immediately without protest if I request it.

D. You will undertake not to belittle me in front of our children, either through words or behavior.

Mileva and the two boys left Albert in Berlin and moved back to Zurich, July 29, 1914. The couple remained married in name only until February 14, 1919, when their divorce was officially issued.

---

* *Albert Einstein, Mileva Marić: The Love Letters*, Princeton University Press, 1992
** *Einstein: His Life and Universe*, Walter Isaacson, Simon & Shuster, 2007

Breakdown

Indigo … a fractured consciousness
pierced by successive heart spasms, crippling back pain
is how I recall the years 1916–17.

War years upsetting the order of everything.

From Berlin back to Zurich, a strain financially,
alone with my boys, desperate to make
a warm, stable home.

I offered piano and mathematics lessons to supplement
Albert's contributions, made holiday preparations:
a festive tree, gifts, games, music.

Dear Zurich friends, my confidante, Helene,
provided support and care in this time of unspeakable
brutality from Albert—the dissolution of all joy.

Our son, Hans Albert, confused, unable to reconcile
his father's hostility, withdrew. I begged him, *write your father,*
make plans for visits, but the boy remained despondent, defensive

each time Albert failed to come, broke another promise.
Tete, only six, floated in the buoyancy of childhood,
thrived in the protective attention of his big brother.

Albert had his dalliances even before Elsa. I knew of his flirtations
and rendezvous with Marie and Anneli, old flames from his youth.
I reproached him, forbade it.

He behaved entitled to whatever
affections women offered him.
Our war began.

I retreated to heal, reached deep
to grasp a fading faith in Albert's loyalty
to me, his sons, to anyone.

If my heart were crystal, his infidelity
delivered the first crack; the separation, a core severance;
his demand for divorce, the shattering.

Premonitions

Zurich, 1917

Never doubt the mind's eye—frightening images
or playful ones—what is sensed in flesh and bones.

Someone I know saw a little man riding along a beam of light.

I, too, saw many things—glimpses of future landscapes:
hillsides tiered in lush gardens, all varieties of cacti,
others burned to smoldering debris.
I felt chilling aches ripple my spine, experienced a dread
that could make of me a frozen woman none would notice.

I disregarded visions, intimations—
after all, I'm a scientist, not an occultist.
I confided in Helene, and she, as a loving friend would,
found me in depressions, retrieved me from
circular corridors, opened drapes and doors.
She bolstered me, though
I knew one day Albert would leave.

Our bright beginning, our invincible love
could not defeat the force of such a dark future.
I ignored premonition, swallowed fear until it stalked
and claimed me in this insatiable illness and bedridden hell.

Masterful Malevolence

The twin to intellectual superiority is intellectual aggression—a cutting
condescension, a tongue that blisters the most tender wounds.

Intentional malice, a direct strike where
the victim is most vulnerable.

A precise aim pinpointed with astute mental geometry,
honed by a frightening sensitivity to the core weakness in others.

Albert was a master at this game.
He enjoyed it.

I witnessed the wounding chagrin of my pension girlfriends, other students
at the Polytechnic, anyone he judged beneath him—
the bourgeois, the philistines,

anyone who'd dare defy or discredit him, and finally me, the wife
he wanted to erase, along with her part in his achievements.

Manipulative, dishonest, distrustful, unstable, bitter, crafty, destructive, depressed,
pathologically insecure, suspicious, passive, miserable, needy, ugly. *

His words written to our Zurich friends to poison their good opinions
of me, justify his abandonment, exonerate himself,

create a cabal of defense against these precise traits in him.
It was not me he saw in this mirror.

I had not only adultery to claim but evidence of my authorship in things
most precious to him. For this he would denounce me as crazy.

Dearest Michele Besso and Heinrich Zangger did not credit
his claims and sought to calm his hysteria—
fits I don't doubt were precipitated by the ever-insistent-upon-divorce Elsa.

---

* Compiled from *Mileva Marić Einstein: Life With Albert Einstein*, Radmila Milentijević,
United World Press, 2015

Heartbroken*

You must abide by stillness, be as still
as a corpse, let the blue cotton cushion you,
silence the sun with shuttered sight.

You must breathe deeply and ever so slowly,
elongated breaths—the rising
and falling of your chest imperceptible.

You must follow your breath inward,
gather debris, sweep up dust,
and follow again outward.

You must count breaths,
days, months, years
until numbers blur and time curves.

The shattering is complete, the
stained glass of your story lies broken
like a galaxy of dead stars at your feet.

If you move, you will be cut again,
bleed again. If you resist,
you will die.

Abide by stillness, soothe the heart
that strikes you, the spine
that will not bend.

Never deny your love for he who cast you aside,
stoned you as if a heretic, he who would
extinguish your spirit if you did not love him so.

---

* In 1916, Albert requested a divorce. Mileva suffered a complete physical and
emotional breakdown and was periodically hospitalized or convalesced at home
over the next two and a half years.

III

Nobel Blackmail

He used that illustrious prize as bait
to hook the divorce he wanted so desperately.

Two years of brutal badgering before his final
offer succeeded for the solvency it would
grant me as much for the admission of my part
in his opus.

Two years more before the award would be conferred
and for him to defy our contract.*

This time I did not take to my bed, but gathered up
those precious papers of his fame, papers
weighted with my research, equations, and proofs—
the indelible papers signed by an invisible hand.

He soon honored the divorce decree though not without
a horrid admonishing of truth in memory,
a memory we never spoke of again.

I purchased three fine houses in Zurich,
raised my sons. My spine grew strong and carried me forward.

Albert became the bourgeois bore he abhorred—
a famous one nevertheless—supplementing his mediocrity
with sensual superfluity.

---

* The Divorce Decree, February 14, 1919, stipulated that the principal (121,572.54 Swedish kronor, or $32,250.00 dollars) of the Nobel Prize become the property of Mileva and be deposited in trust in a Swiss bank, giving her access to the interest. Albert attempted to deposit the capital in a New York bank, and later, to alter the terms of the Divorce Decree in his Last Will.

Genius / Madness

Another
of the great polarities.

A delicate balance
sustains equilibrium
for a measured time before
the scale tips into madness
and the brilliance of genius
dims with candlelight
melting into wax.

Hans grew into a man
of practical applied intelligence,
a mechanical engineer to bring function
and beauty to everyday life.
He's his mother's child.

Tete, my lost boy,
is his father's genius
without gravity.

Novi Sad, 24 February 1922

Papa died today
a disheartened man
stripped of wealth and standing
by war.
Mother ill,
a son missing in Russia,
a mentally dysfunctional daughter,
and me—
his hope and sacrifice,
his prodigy,
who would make history,
his aspiring scientist
lost to motherhood, domesticity,
and the world as it is.

I'm so sorry, Papa.

Hans Albert & Frieda*

I've become my mother-in-law, Pauline,
to judge my son's choice for a wife, disparage
his love for her, criticize her physique and care of him.

The conditions of his work compromise his health,
not she. Hans is happy, as Albert once was with me.

How quickly the old prejudices return.
Albert and I, united in our opposition to her, grow closer.

I wonder, am I honest in my intent,
or do I use my son to win back a husband gone?

---

* Hans Albert married Frieda Knecht on May 7, 1927. The young couple lived
in Dortmund—Germany's industrial Ruhr Valley, where Hans worked as an
engineer, designing bridges.

In His Travels

Albert stays with us in my Zurich home.
We are again a family with
music, company, conversation, our sons.

We again defy social convention,
now as a naughty divorced couple—"The Einsteins."
Who will protest?

Our bond is not sexual. I'm well past that hook and sinker,
yet I often think of Elsa, the compromises she makes
for his freedom and excesses.

She is perhaps a more generous woman than I
or more self-effacing.
His visits bring me joy. I am again whole.

Kindred Spirits

After divorce, a calm,
relief from battles, opposing wills.
He rests; I heal.

The boys are the glue that binds us,

yet there is a greater force, invisible, eternal,
that insists upon transformation, harmony,
and will not let go.

You cannot lose what belongs to you.
This too is a universal law.

Tete*

My poor boy is lost in the abyss
between brilliance and insanity,
a lacuna as yet unnamed.

He tunnels from one reality to another without awareness,
vanishes in fits of rage, ridicule; grasps for anything tangible:
poetry, music, the sound of his own voice.

He's swallowed as if by quicksand.
I alone hear his muffled cries for help.

I know the place that takes him, and will go there, each time, every time,
find his tender hand, meet the terror in his eyes, and lead him back.

I will not lose another child.

---

* Eduard Einstein, Tete (1910–1965), was diagnosed with schizophrenia in 1930
and spent most of his adult life in and out of psychiatric clinics and sanatoriums.

Last Parting, 1933

Nazis, Jews.
A vacuous darkness swallows Europe,
exiles my Albert to America.

I'm again bereft,
though he promises financial support, letters,
to never forsake his Zurich family.

I wonder, *will we see each other again before
we die?*

Schizophrenic

He rides the pendulum between
lethargy and agitation;
the wider the swing, the deeper and longer
the seizure against sanity.

His eyes blacken, grow fierce.
An animal's glint
fixes on a common object—
bed slippers, a doorknob.
Shoulders gather, head drops to aim.
He launches into a fiendish hell, rupturing
the divide between. A storm ensues, a panic-stricken
panther is unleashed. The walls of the house shake,
the very air itself trembles.

I can no longer take care of him.

Pathological

Albert claims I'm mistrustful
in a pathological way, that it's
inherited from my family,
manifested to an incurable
degree in Tete.

Though I speak kindly of Albert,
will never break his trust,
I say to the ghosts, heartbreak,
and bitterness in his wake,
who is pathological?

I say to the world that exalts him,
what pathology denies a woman's mind
or that she could traverse Galileo, Kepler, and Newton
to match his mind, bend light with thought,
and enter the enigma of gravity, time, and space?

No*

Mother, gone in 1935, sister Zorka, 1938,
the same year Hans Albert and family gone to America,
Tete, gone to illness.

1940, another fall, a stone stairway, broken foot,
injured head and spine.

I'm again a bedridden hag
and Tete alone without my visits.

The war, Nazis, death, suffering, money,
never enough money; if an invasion, no escape,
debts, loss, chaos.

Albert, where is Albert?

1944, Helene, dearest friend, the kindest woman
of my life, gone.

1947. A lonely old woman limps home
as if in fog, unable to discern her footing
in space or time—what has happened to her life,
her imprint in history?

Perhaps it's true, all things exist simultaneously—
experience closed only by the senses five—until
another dimension winks and opens.

Another fall,
the one she knew would eventually kill her
even if she refused to go.

---

* Alone in a clinic on the last day of her life, Mileva repeated a single word, *No*.

Old World

Say my deformity made me a shy, introverted girl,
my arrogance, a cold stubborn student,
my carelessness, a bereaved mother.

Say my intellectual limitations failed me as a scientist,
my demands drove Albert away.

Say I couldn't possibly have conceived relativity.

I say the hard-iron, double-standard shackles of men
offer such poor opinions of me.

Zurich, 1948*

Her eyes reflect in window glass, pupils glisten
with want and waiting for him—her Albert,
her *Johnnie*, to round the street corner

to their rooms on *Kramgasse* 49, Bern, their first home
as a distinguished married couple,
a short tram ride from the Patent Office or pub.

She listens for the crowing cock with whimsical bears,
the clamoring chimes of the grand clock tower,
anticipates his arrival, sometimes mirrored

in rain pools, cast in shadow
by late afternoon sun or streetlight.
She'd know his form and gait anywhere.

Waiting was a bottomless lake,
as was losing herself in him. How could she not?
She loved him more than she could love herself.

This evening her eyes, tired and ringed,
reflect in window glass on
a spring evening in Zurich, where

she sits in her favorite upholstered chair.
And this too is a bottomless lake
where memory floats with silver fish and faraway stars.

---

* Mileva Marić Einstein suffered a stroke that paralyzed her left side in May 1948, was hospitalized and died in the EOS Clinic in Zurich, August 4, 1948. She was 73 years old.

Bibliography

Albert Einstein, Mileva Marić: The Love Letters. Edited by Jürgen Renn and Robert Schulmann. Translated by Shawn Smith. Princeton, NJ, Princeton University Press, 1992.

Asmodelle, Estelle. *The Collaboration of Mileva Marić and Albert Einstein, Asian Journal of Physics*, Vol. 24, No. 4, March 2015. https://arxiv.org/pdf/1503.08020. pdf

Gagnon, Pauline. *The Forgotten Life of Einstein's First Wife, Scientific American Guest Blog*, December 19, 2016. https://blogs.scientificamerican.com/guest-blog/the-forgotten-life-of-einsteins-first-wife/

Isaacson, Walter. *Einstein: His Life and Universe.* New York, NY, Simon & Schuster, 2007.

Milentijević, Radmila. *Mileva Marić Einstein: Life with Albert Einstein.* New York, NY, United World Press, 2015.

Overbye, Dennis. *Einstein in Love: A Scientific Romance.* New York, NY, Penguin Books, 2000.

Popović, Milan. *In Albert's Shadow: The Life and Letters of Mileva Marić, Einstein's First Wife.* Baltimore and London, The John Hopkins University Press, 2003.

Acknowledgments

Grateful thanks to the editors of the publications in which the following poems first appeared, sometimes in slightly different form:

Backstory Of The Poem: "Heartbroken"
Muddy River Poetry Review: "Liebe"
Nixes Mate Review: "The Tug of Gravity"
Peacock Journal: "Stepping Stone," "Thought Experiments / Sex," "Elsa,"
      "Premonitions," "Old World"
Writing In A Woman's Voice: "After Lieserl," "Don't Misunderstand," "Mileva,"
      "Novi Sad, 24 February 1922"

Gratitude to Leah Maines of Finishing Line Press for giving Mileva's story a home, to the Stone Ridge Library Writers for their critical feedback and support, to my steadfast family and friends, to Karen Neuberg, Beate Sigriddaughter, José Sotolongo, and Susan Tepper for their gracious words of praise, to Dennis Overbye, whose research and travels for his 2000 biography *Einstein in Love* first brought Mileva to my attention, and to Mileva Marić Einstein, whose resilience and beauty inspired this book.

Copyediting by Cindy Hochman of "100 Proof" Copyediting Services.

Other Books by Catherine Arra

(Women in Parentheses) (2019)
Writing in the Ether (2018)
Tales of Intrigue & Plumage (2017)
Loving from the Backbone (2015)
Slamming & Splitting (2014)

About the Author

Catherine Arra is a former high school English and writing teacher. Since leaving the classroom in 2012, her poetry and prose have appeared in numerous literary journals online and in print, and in several anthologies. She is the author of (*Women in Parentheses*) (Kelsay Books, 2019), *Writing in the Ether* (Dos Madres Press, 2018) and three chapbooks, *Tales of Intrigue & Plumage* (FutureCycle Press, 2017), *Loving from the Backbone* (Flutter Press, 2015), and *Slamming & Splitting* (Red Ochre Press, 2014). Arra is a native of the Hudson Valley in upstate New York, where she lives most of the year, teaches part-time, and facilitates local writing groups. In winters she migrates to the Space Coast of Florida. Find her at www.catherinearra.com.

www.ingramcontent.com/pod-product-compliance
Lightning Source LLC
Chambersburg PA
CBHW021205090426
42740CB00008B/1239